LIVE YOUR LIFE INSURANCE
An Age-Old Approach Revitalized

Kim D. H. Butler

Foreword by Bobby Mattei
R.S. Mattei & Company, Inc.
www.My-MountainTops.com

Live Your Life Insurance © 2008, 2009 by Kim D.H. Butler

All rights reserved. No part of this book may be used or reproduced in any manner whatsoever without written permission, except for brief quotations in critical articles and reviews.

MountainTopsEducation.com
22790 Hwy 259 South
Mt. Enterprise, TX 75681

Prosperity Pathway and Prosperity Principles are trademarks of Partners for Prosperity, Inc.

First print edition. Produced in the United States of America.

To order this book, visit www.My-MountainTops.com or call 318-861-2552.

This publication is designed to provide accurate and authoritative information in regard to the subject matter covered. It is sold with the understanding that the publisher is not engaged in rendering legal, accounting, or other professional services through the content of this publication or with regard to its readers' specific circumstances. If you require legal advice or other expert assistance, you should seek the services of a competent professional through the person who referred you to this book.

Contents

Foreword v

Introduction vii

Part 1: Living with Your Cash Value (CLUE) 1

   Phase 1 — The Start-Up Phase (Years 1–5).................... 2

   Phase 2 — Leverage Opportunity and Investment Capability (Years 6–30)................... 5

   Capsule Concepts — How One Dollar Can Do Many Jobs 9

Part 2: Using Your Death Benefit While You Are Alive 13

   Phase 3 — Spending Other Assets (Years 20–40) 13

   Phase 4 — Using the Death Benefit or Face Value (Years 41–50)...................................... 17

   Phase 5 — Setting Up the Family Bank (Years 51+) 23

Part 3: Glossary — Working Parts Definitions *(Very Important to Learn)* 25

Conclusion — Not Just Any Old Final Page *(You'll Want to Read This)* 37

Additional Reading 41

About the Author 42

Foreword

It is refreshing to hear another voice that understands and articulates how to live, utilize, and benefit from life insurance while you are living. In the past thirty years I have not met anyone with Kim's depth of knowledge and the ability to share direction, confidence and create new capabilities the way she does.

"Why would anyone own whole life insurance?" is always asked. The question presumes that whole life insurance is bad, that this (100 year old) product has no purpose, other than if you die. This so called "bad product", labeled by the media and the majority of typical financial planners, contains incredible properties for prosperity. Additionally, it is necessary for some of the most magnificent, unpublished wonders in the financial world when combined with other assets, while you are living.

Consumers, the "drive-by" media, and typical financial planners have a great capacity to quickly declare something good, or bad, without knowing the facts. After reading this book you will have a good working knowledge of why life insurance is used by essentially every successful bank and Major Corporation in the United States. Think about that last statement. The largest banks in the country currently have more in Life Insurance Cash Value than they do in Bank premises and fixed assets according to the FDIC. Even smaller, non-publicly-traded, local, non-TARP recipient banks, have millions and millions in Life Insurance Cash Values insuring their employees.

This book teaches you how to do the things that financial institutions do and not what they tell you to do.

Finally, I am grateful to have collaborated with Kim and her husband Todd Langford over the years. So enjoy this book, and pay attention. This is real wisdom from a true leader.

Bobby Mattei
R.S. Mattei & Company, Inc.
www.My-MountainTops.com
318-861-2552

Introduction

It's odd that talking about life insurance is mostly a discussion about death. Who wants to talk about death? No one! So even though this book talks about life insurance, it is a book about life and *living* — living with, using, and benefiting from your life insurance while you are living.

This presentation is largely conceptual, since the specifics of everybody's numbers will be different. However, the concepts presented are applicable to a wide variety of financial situations.

Life insurance is one of the oldest financial products around, yet is also one of the most misunderstood. People debate its efficacy from every angle, but rarely is it championed. That is, until recently. After twenty years of business inside the financial services industry, we are just now seeing a few positive notes in the press about whole life insurance being a good place to store money. It also is interesting to note that Roth IRAs are a hot topic. However, life insurance, which is governed by similar tax law, is liquid and is not tied up until age $59 \frac{1}{2}$. This is one of the many reasons that people who own, use, and live their life insurance love it.

This book is about the two oldest types of life insurance known to man: whole life and term insurance. We acknowledge that universal life, variable universal life, and equity indexed universal life may work, but we don't address them for the following reasons:

- No guaranteed premium (how much you pay can vary, both up and down)
- No guaranteed cash value (whole life has a new floor set every year)

- Only a guaranteed interest rate (which means nothing if your account has no money)
- No guaranteed death benefit without an extra charge
- Mortality assumptions that can change and are very difficult to understand
- Lack of proof that they work on a long-term basis
- Under-funding promoted as a way to lessen the cost of the insurance... we ask, if the life insurance is good and helpful to you, why do you want to put the least amount in it?

We've split *Live Your Life Insurance* into three sections:

1. How to use your cash value
2. How to use your death benefit while you are living
3. A glossary of the working parts of the policy

We also tell stories about each of the five phases in the policy. Regardless of your age, you can still start at the beginning, but you might skip a few of the middle phases and then implement the later ones.

Please note: This concept can help men and women of all ages, health situations, and financial backgrounds; it is only limited by your imagination. You simply begin with monthly payments tailored to your capability. There is no lump-sum requirement to start, and you don't have to be insurable. Additionally, as long as you don't cancel the policy, under current tax law, there won't be any income taxes on cash value, death benefits, or money borrowed against them, and loans against the cash value are never on your credit report. If the tax laws change, you still get all the other benefits.

We also discuss the product called life insurance (notice it's not called death insurance) from a Human Life Value approach, not a "needs" approach. Human Life Value (HLV), according to Solomon Huebner, is "the value of your future earnings." Many life insurance companies use various parameters to evaluate this, such as fifteen times your income or one times your net worth. Everyone has HLV, even if they are stay-at-home parents or retired volunteers living only on social security payments. You are important in this world, and HLV is only one way to measure that importance economically.

Insuring yourself for your full Human Life Value changes throughout your life. It is important for your family, but also for your own use. In this book, we also discuss how to use your life insurance death benefit (not just the cash) while you are living, to increase cash flow and make better use of the assets you have built along the way.

The needs-analysis approach, so often used in the life insurance industry, is mathematically incorrect. Insurance is designed to indemnify or "make whole" something that is missing. For example, if you drive a $50,000 car, you insure it for $50,000 — not what you "need" to insure it for, because you only "need" to drive a car worth maybe $20,000. With car or home insurance, there is no assuming of various interest rates and inflation rates, nor attempting to perform a "needs analysis," yet it's done with life insurance all the time. *You* don't "need" life insurance, your family does, but you can *use* life insurance, especially since the triggering event is *guaranteed*. Because death is guaranteed, you know there will be a benefit from the insurance as long as it is in force when you die. No other insurance works this way. No one wants a guarantee that they'll use their car, home, liability, or even disability insurance. We're sure no one wants a guarantee they'll use their life insurance either, but if you follow the guidance here you can *live* your life insurance.

Most people fulfill their Human Life Value with a mix of whole life and term insurance, since funding their entire HLV with whole life insurance may be a big step to take. One idea is to take full HLV now, with part of it being whole life and part of it being term, and then convert the term to whole life as you go. Most companies offer conversion credits, so you'll possibly get a little of your money back and have the full amount of coverage all along the way. Plus, on the occasion where a major health change occurs, you are already approved and the insurance company can't take the term insurance away from you while you are converting (as long as it's before the term's time frame ends). **Interesting note:** Most companies will allow you to convert your term insurance to whole life if *they* are the ones who have to start paying the premium due to disability and if the waiver of premium provision is on the policy (see glossary G). This should tell us something about which of these policies is less expensive in the long run.

There is nothing wrong with term insurance for a period of time (hence the name, term insurance). Just understand that it rarely pays a death benefit. It's been widely quoted that only a small percentage of term insurance actually stays on the books long enough to pay a claim. So "Which is better, term or whole life?" should be replaced with the question "How can I protect my full Human Life Value *and* take advantage of what whole life provides?"

And since "questions are infinitely more valuable than answers," according to Dan Sullivan, owner of The Strategic Coach, there will be questions throughout the book to get you thinking. Some of them even have answers. Then the fun begins—combining all the concepts together is what really makes life insurance *live*.

So "keep your mind wide open" (as Anna Sophia Robb sings in the theme song of the movie *The Bridge to Terabithia*) and let's begin a journey through a life filled with living your life insurance.

Part 1: Living with Your Cash Value

Many people view life insurance as a black hole where money goes and that someday someone gets a benefit and it isn't you; or worse, you pay for years, then see nothing. *This is incorrect.* Once you learn how to live your life insurance, you'll see that it's a perfect place to store cash that you will use for financing vehicles and other assets, as well as investment opportunities. The CLUE method of a dividend-paying, whole life insurance policy is so valuable that almost everybody should own one for their own benefit. Notice we said "own"… which doesn't necessarily mean the insurance is on you, but rather that you own and control it. You can own insurance on anyone for whom you have an "insurable interest" — a child, a business partner, a key employee, or anyone so close to you that if they died, you would be affected. This enables everyone (even those who have a thick medical file and may be uninsurable) to benefit from this concept.

So how to do you get a CLUE?

The CLUE Method is an instrumental part of the principles in this e-book. We'll discuss it in more detail later on (see D in the glossary), but for now let's introduce the concept and its parts.

C = Control

L = Liquidity

U = Use

E = Equity

The cash value is your CLUE account. Cash value

and death benefit are 100% in *control* of the owner (not the insured), and the cash value is 100% *liquid*. You (the owner) can *use* both the cash value and the death benefit while you are living, and they work like *equity* in real estate — with one major exception: they can never go down, only up.

PHASE 1 — The Start-Up Phase (Years 1-5)

This is the hardest part, deciding you want to adopt this more effective but less known way of handling your finances. It's like starting a business; not only do you have to work against the nay-sayers, but you have to write checks, write checks, write checks, and only *then* do you see any benefit.

During this phase, you are converting cash to cash value plus a death benefit. Both can provide tax-free income when used properly. And both are wonderful things to have, but hard to start. However, one start-up (though you may have many) equals a lifetime of benefits.

It's very important to remember that "you finance everything you buy." This quotation from Nelson Nash, author of *Becoming Your Own Banker*, indicates the accurate but rarely discussed fact that you either pay interest to someone for the use of their money or you give up interest you could have earned by using your own money. Life insurance gives you a way to more effectively finance the things you buy.

Ben & Bernie's Story: Starting Up… A Challenge

A young couple named Ben and Bernie learned about

Live Your Life Insurance and invested every spare dollar in three different policies. They stuck with the strategy they had committed to, even though their friends and parents thought they were crazy. They suffered through the first few years of premium payments with no reward — but then the policy exploded like popcorn. It formed the foundation that allowed them to invest in everything they wanted to for the rest of their lives. The life insurance didn't make them rich, but everything else they were free to invest in did. It was the foundation of the life insurance that helped all their real estate deals work when they weren't cash-flowing by themselves. It was the life insurance that supported them while the stock market was on one of its many of its roller coaster rides. And it was the cash value of their life insurance that supported them through a couple of down years in their business and gave them a place to store liquid cash in the good times.

Mark & Mary's Story: Starting Up and Keeping Going

Mark and Mary were good savers and had been putting money into his 401(k), dollar-cost-averaging into mutual funds, and faithfully paying their life insurance premiums. When his income decreased due to company restructuring, they dropped their dollar-cost-averaging approach. Around the same time, they moved so their daughter could attend a better school, and since their company wasn't matching their 401(k) contributions, they were debating dropping those as well. (Money was getting tighter every month.)

They called us, concerned that the only money they would be saving was their life insurance premiums, which were now equal to 15 percent of their gross income. We looked at their policy and identified that, for every dollar they put in, the cash value was growing by a dollar and twelve cents, since they were in their fourth year and had not added any manual paid-up additions.

Mark acknowledged the $10,000 he had put in his 401(k) had actually gone down to $9,000, so one dollar was turning into 90 cents during that year. He knew that this may or may not continue the roller coaster ride. Mary had been wanting to start saving for her daughter's education and realized they could use the life insurance cash value to pay for her college just as well, if not better, than a government 529 plan. She remembered the concept of lost opportunity cost (see section "O" in the glossary) and knew if they used the 529 plan they would lose the opportunity for that money to contribute to their retirement funds. Conversely, if they used the life insurance cash value, they could borrow against it *and*, since it would keep growing, it would be able to contribute to their financial independence later on as well.

Phase 1 Questions for You to Think About:

1. How could you get your own policy started?
2. Who could you use for the insured while you were the owner, if that's a better arrangement for your situation?
3. What assets or cash-flow streams of yours might be better placed through a life insurance policy than where they currently are?

PHASE 2 — The Leverage Opportunity Phase and Investment Capability Phase (Years 6-30)

This is the enabler phase. It can begin as early as year 2 or as late as you like. Life insurance enables you to make better use of the game of financing (cars, vacations, etc.), as well as to make better investment decisions. Now that you are past the start-up phase, you can see that every dollar you put into your policy is turning into more than one dollar of cash value. This gives you opportunities for leverage and capabilities for investments.

Victor's Story: What Happens If I Can't Pay My Premium?

Victor had just completed the two-year mark on his policy when his business slowed and he asked for an automatic premium loan (APL). (See M in the glossary.) He knew this would allow him to stop paying premiums out of his pocket, yet keep the money he had put in there and enable it to still grow while borrowing against it for the premium, literally recycling the money. Since there wasn't quite enough money in the policy for a month's premium, $530, we asked the insurance company for an APL for $500 and he wrote a check for $30. The next month, the cash value had increased by $500 (and he had a loan for $500) and he wrote another check for $30. This went on for about five months until he hit his policy anniversary date.

He paid the interest out of pocket for the next twelve months on the $2,500 he had borrowed (at 8 percent it equaled $200) and then kept borrowing against the cash value to pay the premium. And during this twelve months, for every $530 he borrowed, his cash value increased by $610, so he could borrow against it again — thus increasing the loan and increasing the cash value at the same time. A year later, his business picked back up again, so he started paying his own premium. Then, as he was able, he paid off the loan in larger lump sums when he had the cash. This built his policy back up so he could borrow again in a time of need or for an investment opportunity.

Kelly & Katie's Story: Leverage Opportunities

Kelly and Katie had just borrowed against their policy for the first time to buy a new car when Kelly lost his job. Katie was at home with their babies and he wanted to be doing outside sales. It was a huge relief to them *not* to have to make payments for awhile. Then, in his new job, when commissions started up, he paid extra to replace the borrowed funds. They ended up with a paid-off car, a paid-off (life insurance cash-value) loan, and quite a bit of cash because the value of their policy kept growing even though it had a loan against it.

Sam & Sarah's Story: Investment Capability

Sam and Sarah had bought four policies over the last ten years and borrowed against them to finance cars. They had to move around the country changing employers so often that they hadn't been able to save for retirement in a company-sponsored plan. They knew they'd paid back their car loans, but had forgotten that the policies had also grown quite a bit beyond the payments — they effectively had their own private form of retirement savings. In the end, they got all the cars and all the cash, because they borrowed against the cash value and paid it back, borrowed it again and paid it back again, and again and again.

John & Jane's Story: An Investment Opportunity and Starting a Business

John and Jane had wanted to open a children's toy store for years. He had a sales job and she'd been home with the children while they researched various options. Finally, with a loan from the bank, they got started on their first store. It'd been open for about a year when an opportunity came along for a second store, but the bank wouldn't give them a second loan for the additional inventory. Their return on investment in the first store was over 20 percent, so they felt they could do the same in the new store if they could just get the inventory. They'd been faithfully funding their life insurance for seven years and were quite surprised to be reminded how quickly and easily they could borrow against the cash value. They opened their second store, after buying the inventory it needed, and began paying back the life insurance loan from the sales right away (since it was summer and sales were high). When winter came along after Christmas and sales were slow, they took a break from the payments and then resumed them again the next summer. After three summers of diligent loan payments, the loan against the cash value was paid off and they were able to use the cash value again for another investment.

Tom's Story: Investing with Borrowed Cash Value

Tom loved real estate, but due to limited time he couldn't invest in it directly — so he chose to borrow against his cash value and put the money to use to make a higher return. While this may not be a strategy for everyone, he had real estate contacts and confidence in this series of steps, and the ideas may stimulate your own thinking. He borrowed against his cash value, paying 8 percent to use the life insurance company's money while his own cash value kept on growing. He then loaned this money to a bridge-loan broker and was able to find a 14 percent loan to invest in. (Again, not for everyone.) Since he had borrowed to invest, he was able to deduct the 8 percent against the 14 percent. Life insurance loan interest isn't always deductible. However, if the loan is used for a business purpose or investments and you can prove it, then the interest is deductible against the earnings from the investment (but not typically against earned income, so you'll want to check with your CPA on this issue). Every month when his investment gave him an interest payment, he paid it to the life insurance company. Over time, his life insurance cash-value loan was paid off and he still had his investment. The downside of this strategy is that if he had lost the money in the investment, he would still owe the life insurance company the money he had borrowed.

Phase 2 Questions for You to Think About:

1. What loans do you now have that could be restructured to take advantage of borrowing against your policy's cash value instead of from a bank?

2. What investment opportunities have you found that need a lump sum of money, yet you only have the ability to save a smaller amount every month?

3. Could starting a life insurance policy enable

you to do what you can now monthly while you build up the lump sum?

Capsule Concepts in Part 1

Borrowing and receiving dividends (if left in the policy) are tax-free events.

The CLUE Method

C = Control

Start flowing money to yourself in an account you control instead of away from yourself in accounts you don't control.

L = Liquidity

Build wealth that cannot be taken away from you by the stock market or the real estate market roller-coaster rides.

U = Use

Save money for later and purchase discretionary items now.

E = Equity

Create an account where you are benefiting from the ability to leverage, in a way that is better than paying cash, because paying cash is losing interest in an investment. (See glossary O: Lost Opportunity Cost.)

Process to borrow
1. Call your insurance company or financial advisor.
2. Request the loan. (There is no approval process.)
3. Sign one form so they know it's you.
4. Receive your money in ten days.

Process to pay back
1. Choose the method and time frame. (AGAIN, YOU CHOOSE THIS.)
2. Pay back interest only, OR
3. Make month payments of principal and interest, OR
4. Make quarterly payments of principal only, OR
5. Make lump sum payments of principal only.

How do I get my money to do more than one job?

Most people have each of their dollars only doing one job — retirement funding, educating their children, paying off their mortgage, etc. However, once you've learned how to live your life insurance, you can see how easy it is to get one dollar to do many jobs.

So, as we close our cash-value section, let's see how life insurance is similar to real estate and how the two together can get one dollar to do eighteen or more jobs. Real estate ownership has eight main characteristics:

1. Mortgage payments
2. Property
3. Potential appreciation
4. Depreciation (if it's investment real estate, which gives you tax advantages)

5. Cash flow
6. Disposition
7. Leverage
8. Stepped-up basis to heirs (no tax)

Life insurance also has eight main characteristics that are very similar:

1. Premium payments (which, like mortgage payments, are one of the few things benefited by inflation)
2. Cash value
3. Death benefit
4. Waiver of premium
5. Increasing death benefit
6. Paid-up addition capability
7. Leverage
8. Income tax-free to heirs

Both real estate and life insurance also grow and can ultimately be "sold" with minimal tax liability, as indicated by the eighth characteristic. So, if you can borrow against your life insurance to buy real estate and use your real estate to pay back your life insurance loans, you've got one dollar doing about twenty to twenty-three jobs. You don't have to combine life insurance and real estate to get one dollar to do many jobs, but the two do work very similarly and the above is just an example. Furthermore, if you add the ways to *use* your death benefit while living, which we'll cover in the next section, you add at least five or six more jobs.

Part 2:
Using Your Death Benefit While You Are Alive

PHASE 3 — Spending Other Assets (Years 20-40)

This is the cross-over between Part 1 and Part 2, between using your cash value as a cash account to borrow against and using your death benefit to borrow against. Typical ages of those insured during this phase are the 60s, 70s, and 80s, and how you use your life insurance at this point will depend on how long you've had it, as well as how many dollars are currently borrowed against it.

> *"The first beneficiary of a life insurance policy should be the owner."*
>
> — Bob Ball, trainer extraordinaire to life insurance agents nationwide

If you knew that when you reached age 80 or so you would be given a large sum of money or a guaranteed stream of income that would last the rest of your life, would you act differently between ages 60 and 80?

Of course you would! You might do any or all of the following:

A. Spend down the rest of your assets

B. Mortgage or reverse-mortgage your home

C. Give away more to charity to increase your tax deductions

... and in doing any of these, you'd be living your life insurance.

Now, let's look more closely at strategy A (illustrated in Table 1 on the next page):

We have two theoretical couples of similar ages, with the same set of investment products purchased over the years, culminating in the following scenario. All four people are age 60, with each couple having $1 million of paid-up whole life insurance, a $3,000-per-month pension, $1 million of real estate equity, and $1 million of taxable certificates of deposits. They are in the 35% tax bracket.

From ages 60–80, "The Prosperity Couple" on the left spends down their CDs so they are gone by age 80, uses their life insurance, is confident and thinking from abundance, and at age 80, places their home (they wanted to downsize) in a charitable remainder trust, increasing their income and yet insuring their children get some cash at their death.

From ages 60–80, "The Poverty Couple" on the right takes only interest off their CDs, ignores their life insurance, is fearful and thinking from scarcity, and at age 80, would like to give more to charity but are afraid of running out of money and having to rely on their children and don't want to sell their "large" home for fear of paying so much in capital gains tax.

From ages 60–80, The Prosperity Couple has $732,147 more income over the 21-year period. (See far right column.)

Distribution

Account Value: 1,000,000
Earnings Rate: 5.00%
EOY Withdrawal: (77,996)
Withdrawal Increase: 0.00%
Tax On Earnings

Illustration Period: 21
State Income Tax: 0.00%
Federal Tax Bracket: 35.00%

Tax Credit For Losses

Account Value: 1,000,000
Earnings Rate: 5.00%
EOY Withdrawal: (50,000)
Withdrawal Increase: 0.00%
Tax On Earnings

Year	Beg. Of Year Acct. Value	Earnings Rate	Gross Withdrawal	Tax Payment	Net Spendable	Beg. Of Year Acct. Value	Earnings Rate	Gross Withdrawal	Tax Payment	Net Spendable	Compare Dist.1-Dist.2
1	1,000,000	5.00%	(77,996)	(17,500)	60,496	1,000,000	5.00%	(50,000)	(17,500)	32,500	27,996
2	972,004	5.00%	(77,996)	(17,010)	60,986	1,000,000	5.00%	(50,000)	(17,500)	32,500	28,486
3	942,608	5.00%	(77,996)	(16,496)	61,500	1,000,000	5.00%	(50,000)	(17,500)	32,500	29,000
4	911,742	5.00%	(77,996)	(15,955)	62,041	1,000,000	5.00%	(50,000)	(17,500)	32,500	29,541
5	879,333	5.00%	(77,996)	(15,388)	62,608	1,000,000	5.00%	(50,000)	(17,500)	32,500	30,108
6	845,304	5.00%	(77,996)	(14,793)	63,203	1,000,000	5.00%	(50,000)	(17,500)	32,500	30,703
7	809,573	5.00%	(77,996)	(14,168)	63,829	1,000,000	5.00%	(50,000)	(17,500)	32,500	31,329
8	772,055	5.00%	(77,996)	(13,511)	64,485	1,000,000	5.00%	(50,000)	(17,500)	32,500	31,985
9	732,662	5.00%	(77,996)	(12,822)	65,175	1,000,000	5.00%	(50,000)	(17,500)	32,500	32,675
10	691,299	5.00%	(77,996)	(12,098)	65,898	1,000,000	5.00%	(50,000)	(17,500)	32,500	33,398
11	647,868	5.00%	(77,996)	(11,338)	66,658	1,000,000	5.00%	(50,000)	(17,500)	32,500	34,158
12	602,265	5.00%	(77,996)	(10,540)	67,456	1,000,000	5.00%	(50,000)	(17,500)	32,500	34,956
13	554,382	5.00%	(77,996)	(9,702)	68,294	1,000,000	5.00%	(50,000)	(17,500)	32,500	35,794
14	504,105	5.00%	(77,996)	(8,822)	69,174	1,000,000	5.00%	(50,000)	(17,500)	32,500	36,674
15	451,315	5.00%	(77,996)	(7,898)	70,098	1,000,000	5.00%	(50,000)	(17,500)	32,500	37,598
16	395,884	5.00%	(77,996)	(6,928)	71,068	1,000,000	5.00%	(50,000)	(17,500)	32,500	38,568
17	337,682	5.00%	(77,996)	(5,909)	72,087	1,000,000	5.00%	(50,000)	(17,500)	32,500	39,587
18	276,570	5.00%	(77,996)	(4,840)	73,156	1,000,000	5.00%	(50,000)	(17,500)	32,500	40,656
19	212,403	5.00%	(77,996)	(3,717)	74,279	1,000,000	5.00%	(50,000)	(17,500)	32,500	41,779
20	145,027	5.00%	(77,996)	(2,538)	75,458	1,000,000	5.00%	(50,000)	(17,500)	32,500	42,958
21	74,282	5.00%	(77,996)	(1,300)	76,696	1,000,000	5.00%	(50,000)	(17,500)	32,500	44,196
TOTAL	0	5.00%	(1,637,918)	(223,274)	1,414,647	1,000,000	5.00%	(1,050,000)	(367,500)	682,500	732,147

This difference is calculated by looking at The Poverty Couple's interest-only income of 5 percent x $1,000,000 for a $32,500 net income versus The Prosperity Couple's "pay down of principal plus interest" income of $60,496 in the first year growing to $76,696 in the twenty-first year. Obviously, the Poverty Couple will still have their $1,000,000 and the Prosperity Couple won't; however, The Prosperity Couple goes on to use any of the other strategies listed here to continue their income. Also notice in the table on the previous page how much less tax The Prosperity Couple paid due to this pay-down or spend-down strategy.

Now, let's examine strategy B:

At age 80, the couples could also reverse-mortgage their homes to increase their income further. This would be done instead of donating the home to the Charitible Remainder Trust as above so they could keep living in it. (Reverse mortgages provide tax-free income, especially effective when paired with a life insurance policy to pay off the debt upon death.) At age 90, they could start taking out life insurance dividends in cash to offset inflation. And at age 100, they could sell their life insurance policies, if they know their children are financially well off, and if they feel it is more fun to give cash to their grandchildren and great-grandchildren than leave the gifts for after death.

Selling your life insurance policy is typically known as a "Life Settlement." This is done in a confidential, escrow-controlled environment in which investors buy your policy — paying you more money than the insurance company might in net cash value, but less than the death benefit. One might also use a bank or a private individual to accomplish this, basically leveraging the death benefit in advance.

Lastly, let's have a look at strategy C:

Knowing you'll have increased income due to the strategies to be presented in Phase 4, you may choose to give away higher amounts earlier — which would increase your deductions, enabling you to pay less tax and consequently have a higher income.

> "Producers understand the best way to reduce their insurance cost (not price) is to buy as much of it as possible, because every moment you spend worrying about loss is a moment that you are not thinking productively, and that moment cannot be recaptured."
>
> — *Killing Sacred Cows* by Garrett Gunderson

Phase 3 Questions for You to Think About:

1. Who do you know who is living only on interest because they are afraid to spend their principle?
2. What steps could you take today so that you could act like The Prosperity Couple?

PHASE 4 — Using the Death Benefit or Face Value (Years 41-50)

There are seven ways you can use your death benefit or face amount while you are living. These can be combined or used as stand-alone strategies. It is interesting to note that life insurance helps people from a wide variety of financial backgrounds. For modest income earners the premium payments become an important strategy for forced savings. Also, medium income earners end up with more dollars saved outside the policy because of the CLUE account flexibility and the lack of a financial roller coaster impacting them. Lastly, life insurance helps those with larger amounts of money as they head into retirement age by enabling them to spend their own assets more efficiently. This last group could have $1 million or $1 billion, but the concepts are still the same.

Following are seven examples of how to use your life insurance death benefit while you are living.

1. THE SPEND-DOWN

Typical retirees spend only interest, leaving their principal in the hands of the financial institutions. Guess who benefits from this? The institutions and the government do, and you don't. See Table 1 on page 15 where we show you how much the government gets in taxes while you leave your principal at the institution in a taxable account. This happens in a tax-deferred account as well; it's just less dramatic since we don't see it happening every year, because the problem is deferred. If instead, you purposely take out interest *and* a portion of principal every year in what is called a spend-down or a pay-down, then you will receive more money, pay less tax, and leave less in control of the financial institution.

This strategy should first occur with all qualified plan monies like 401(k)s and IRAs, as well as any SEPs, Simple IRAs and 401(k)s, and Roths. Believe it or not, the Qualified Plan (IRA, etc.) is the last asset you want to die with. Many advisors recommend continuing to defer these accounts, and for some that may make sense, but every client we've looked at will have more money to spend and more to give away if they will pay down these accounts.

Secondly, spend down all taxable accounts like CDs, money markets, stock accounts, mutual funds, bonds, etc. If you are unsure of your time frames (like the 21 years we used on page 14), we suggest you take an 8 percent withdrawal. Most planners would suggest 4 percent or 6 percent, but this is not sufficient to remove enough principal. If 8 percent won't zero out the account in twenty years or so, then we suggest using an even-higher interest rate.

This spend-down strategy requires a Phase 4 for what to do after you've spent all your money and have no more in liquid accounts. The various options in Phase 4 are the following ways to use your death benefit while you are living. Again, you could use them separately or together. This can be a tricky concept to understand, so get help from someone who can clearly explain it to you before you are ready to make decisions. If you are in your 20s, 30s, or 40s, all you need to remember is: "I can use my life insurance death benefit when I'm in my 80s."

Pat & Pam's Story: Using Their Death Benefit While Living

Pat and Pam drove their ninth brand-new car down the road, talking about how they remember when they learned the most-efficient way to purchase and finance cars, some thirty years earlier. Their bumper sticker read: "We are spending our kid's inheritance and giving it to them, too." As they joined their friends for dinner, Pat explained they were able to use up all their own assets knowing there would be a death benefit left over for the kids and grandchildren.

2. REVERSE MORTGAGE

Implementing a reverse mortgage whereby you get tax-free income from your paid-off (or almost paid-off) home is an efficient use of a lazy asset — if you can see the benefits and stop worrying about paying off your home. Remember, the value of a house is two-fold: a place to live and a potential asset to pass on to your children or grandchildren. So, if you combine a reverse mortgage with life insurance, your cash flow will increase and your heirs will be better off (with more flexibility) after you pass on. This increases your debt and the life insurance death benefit can then pay it off, if you choose, but some people struggle with the moral ramifications of the concept, even though it's been a viable strategy for years. Not all mortgage brokers are familiar with these loans, so look before you jump.

3. TAKE LIFE INSURANCE DIVIDENDS OUT IN CASH NOW

This is a strategy to use later in life. Switch from using dividends to purchase paid-up additions to having them paid out in cash. This can supplement your income, which may mean the difference between a trip in the car and a trip in a plane — or more importantly, the difference between just surviving and really living. The annual dividend can be taken in tax-free cash, up to your basis. "Basis" is defined as the total amount of money you've paid as premiums and paid-up additions. If you exceed your basis, then your dividend (if taken in cash) will be taxable, although you could switch to loans at that time and avoid having the income stream taxed, according to current I.R.S. law. We suggest you still make the premium payment every year to enable the dividend to keep rising and keep up with inflation, but depending on your circumstance, this may not be necessary.

4. PENSION MAXIMIZATION

This suggests a strategy for those of you with defined benefit-style pensions whereby you must make a choice between taking income during just your life (single-life payout) or during two lives (joint-life payout). If you have life insurance in force, you can take the higher payout (single-life), knowing that when you die, your spouse will get the death-benefit money and can turn that into an income stream (to replace what may have been the pension income).

5. LEVERAGING THE BENEFIT BY SELLING IT

The purchaser can be a public company or a private party, or you can use it as collateral. In the first instance, you sell your policy to a life-settlement company, which specializes in buying death benefits for more than the insurance companies pay for them. The amount your insurance company would give you is the "current net cash value surrender amount," which is the cash-value account you've been using all along. The life settlement may be more, depending on your age and health at the time. Likewise, you could do the same with a private party who was willing to take the risk. These two ideas would end your control of the policy in any form.

Lastly, you could also use the death benefit as collateral. Remember, at this point, we are discussing the phase of your policy when you are in your 80s, 90s, or beyond. So, at that age, you could go to a bank or private individual and assign to them some or all of your death benefit in exchange for lending you some cash. This would leave you in control and with the ability to pay them off at any time and gain control over your policy again. Finally, when you die, they would be paid off and your family would receive the rest of the death benefit.

6. THE CHARITABLE REMAINDER TRUST (CRT)

This is a way to sell a highly appreciated asset (like stocks, real estate, or a business) through a charity without paying as much capital gains tax as if you sold it directly. Here's a very simplified CRT process: (1) give the asset to a charity, (2) get a deduction for the gift, (3) let the charity sell the asset, (4) the charity then invests the money and (5) pays you an income stream. When you die, (6) the charity gets the remainder of the money and (7) your family gets the life insurance instead. In this process, step 5 would be the way you'd use your death benefit while you were living. But since most people wouldn't follow this strategy if it meant their family would get nothing, by having your life insurance in place, your family is made "whole" in step 7.

7. ANNUITIZE THE POLICY

Annuitize the policy with the insurance company that is providing it. Most insurance companies will provide this option, but it's one you'd want to do quite late in life as it's irrevocable. You will pick a timeframe: 10 or 20 years, life expectancy, or life plus a certain amount to the beneficiaries. Then, the insurance company will guarantee you a certain amount of income for the timeframe you pick. It would be an alternative to selling it to a third party like a life settlement. It's also a reason why having many smaller policies is actually better than a few large ones, because you can do all seven of these strategies with that number of policies.

Phase 4 Questions for You to Think About:

1. Who do you know sitting in a paid-off home that doesn't have any cash flow to enjoy life?
2. Who do you know getting ready to make a major decision about their pension plan and how to take income from it?
3. Who do you know who owns a life insurance policy and isn't sure what to do with it?
4. Who do you know with a highly appreciated asset, but they're afraid to sell it because of the high tax liability?

PHASE 5 — Setting Up the "Family Bank" (Years 51+)

Ideally, you'll die late in life with (1) most of your assets used up and (2) your entire net worth, at its highest point, paid to your family and charities in the form of an income tax-free death benefit from the life insurance you own. Yes, there might be estate taxes on it, but that's a subject for another e-book. Do remember the "right" amount of life insurance is fifteen times your income or one times your net worth.

With proper estate-planning documentation, this lump sum of cash could create a "family bank" whereby your grandchildren and great-grandchildren could borrow sums of money to pursue opportunities. This is the way wealthy families stay wealthy for generations — they replace their assets at each generation's passing and buy life insurance at each baby's birth.

Your family's bank can have a Board of Directors or Trustees that make loan decisions. Ideally, each borrower should sign promissory notes, pay interest and principle, and generally treat the asset like they would a commercial bank's (penalties included!).

How specific you wish to design your family bank is up to you. And the legal document itself that governs the family bank is generally a changeable trust until you die, at which point it becomes irrevocable. You can also leave specific amounts of the death benefit to charity or particular family members based on your desires.

Phase 5 Questions for You to Think About:

1. Would you like to be able to set up your family with a banking opportunity they can use while you are living as well as when you are gone?

2. Do you have charities you'd like to continue to support after your death?

3. Are you curious about the various ways to use your life insurance while you are living? Then contact the people who suggested this book and they'll show you specific ways that would work for your situation so you could use your life insurance, too.

Part 3: Glossary

Working parts definitions

- A. Premium
- B. Cash value (guaranteed portion)
- C. Dividends that purchase automatic paid-up additions (PUAs)
- D. Gross cash value = (b + c) (though some insurance companies call this net cash value)
- E. Automatic paid-up additions
- F. Manual paid-up additions
- G. Waiver of premium
- H. Death benefit or face amount
- I. Increasing death benefit
- J. Interest charged on borrowed cash value
- K. Owner
- L. Insured
- M. Automatic premium loan (APL)
- N. Reduced paid-up (RPU) policies
- O. Opportunity cost

A. Premium

The monthly or annual payment you make to the insurance company that goes into your account and also pays for the death benefit. It helps self-impose discipline, and helps money move (which is a critical principle in causing it to grow). The effect is that one premium dollar will do at least five jobs: build cash value, create dividends, maintain waiver of premium (see G), increase the death benefit, and provide the ability to leverage.

B. Cash value

For whole life, a guaranteed dollar figure, which is the amount in the account (not a guaranteed interest rate). This account is guaranteed to increase every year, even if the company does not pay a dividend. A new "floor" (minimum) is set annually on your policy anniversary date, and it can never go down as long as either you or your cash value or your dividends are paying premiums.

C. Dividends

An amount paid to you for being an owner of the policy, or if the life insurance company is "mutual" instead of "stock," for being an owner of the company. There are many ways to use dividends; most companies have at least twenty options to choose from and you can change them as often as you like. The best option in the early years is automatic paid-up additions (see E), which automatically increase the cash value, the death benefit, and future dividend-earning capability. The word "dividend" in this context is a confusing term since it does not perform like a stock dividend. Once policy dividends have been paid, they become guaranteed and cannot drop in value. They are not taxable as long as they are left in the policy to buy more paid-up additions (see E). They also are not taxed when borrowed against. And they are not taxed upon withdrawal until you exceed your basis (the amount of premium you've put in plus any manual paid-up additions you've added).

D. Gross cash value

This is B plus C, the amount you can borrow against. This is your account, 100% owned and controlled by you. Recall the CLUE method from page 9: control, liquidity, use, equity.

CONTROL: You own it, you control it, you say when, you say how much, and you say who, how often, and why.

LIQUIDITY: This account is 100% liquid within ten days at most insurance companies. (Note, there may not be much net cash value in the first few years of the policy, but whatever is in there is 100% available.)

USE: Even if you never move a dollar, your cash value account is the single most-efficient and effective place to store money. It's efficient because it grows in a tax-deferred manner (taxable only if you cancel), and it's effective because you can borrow against it while it still grows at the gross value. Both capabilities are not available in 401(k)s and other tax-deferred accounts. In fact, when you die, this cash-value account (now turned death benefit) will pass on to your heirs without any income tax paid at all, under current law. It's the best place to store "peace of mind" money.

EQUITY: Just think real estate. Equity in real estate is leverage-able, you can borrow against it, but the underlying asset just keeps on growing unaffected by the debt. This is the single most misunderstood aspect of this product. You borrow against it, but you don't take it out. The net cash value is what is left over to still borrow. For example, if you have $100,000 of gross cash value and you borrow $40,000, your account will still grow as if it were $100,000, not $60,000. If you are borrowing against your cash value to invest, that interest should be deducted against that investment's earnings. However, if you are borrowing against the cash value to pay premiums (for an Automatic Premium Loan, see M) or go on vacation, then that interest is not deductible.

> **NOTE for E and F:** *The terms "automatic" and "manual" are mine. Insurance companies don't use them, but I have here in order to help you understand what your opportunities are.*

E. Automatic paid-up additions

These are what dividends buy and they do so automatically (assuming you choose this as your dividend election). The dividend purchases a paid-up (meaning no more premiums are due) miniature policy (that gets added to the base policy) that has cash value, dividends and death benefit that all increase annually. Think of it like a raspberry. There is the base of the berry, then each little globule of goody is its own little berry and they grow exponentially in a compound way.

F. Manual paid-up additions

These are cash payments that can be added, on an optional basis. They act in the same way as automatic paid-up additions. Some companies are more flexible with this than others. Some allow monthly payments, others only annual. Some require a little ($100) to keep the door open (use it or lose it), whereas others don't.

Regardless, this is a manual environment, one you control 100 percent within the guidelines of the company and the I.R.S. One important point: There can be too much of a good thing. Add too much money in manual paid-up additions and your life insurance policy (with very effective tax law) will become a Modified Endowment Contract — MEC (with less-than-effective tax law). So make sure you know your particular company's interpretation of the I.R.S. rules and stay within them. This should pique your curiosity: If the I.R.S. set a rule about the maximum amount of money you could put in a certain place, then maybe that place has some value.

G. Waiver of premium (WP)

Not everyone gets approved for this, so if you do, you should accept it. It pays the premium (and sometimes depending on how it's structured, the manual paid-up addition rider as well) if you become disabled for a minimum period of time, depending on the company. The waiting period is usually six months and the payout period often extends to age 60 or 65 with various definitions of disability. This is *not* disability insurance, but rather a rider that will let your life insurance continue growing and having new premiums added to it, if you are disabled and not able to add them yourself. It increases economic certainty because of the "self-completing" nature of the coverage. While premiums are being paid under the WP rider, the cash value and death benefit continues to rise and dividends could be taken in cash to supplement any other income. It's interesting to note that if you have term insurance with WP on it, most insurance companies will allow you to convert to whole life upon disability. What does that say about which is less expensive in the long run?

H. Death benefit or face amount

Death benefit is just what it implies: you die, and the company pays. However, since that chance is statistically unlikely in the early years, we'll just be grateful for the peace of mind that comes from knowing our loved ones will be cared for monetarily if we go early. "Face amount" is just another term for the same thing.

I. Increasing death benefit

In most whole life policies, the death benefit or face amount increases every year. This benefit can be defined by one word: inflation. With medical and scientific advances, it's possible some of you will live 100 more years. You might think 5 percent inflation is high; however, we aren't talking about the government standard here, but your standard — for which things like travel, top-notch medical care, and schooling increase at a much faster pace. You'll want your death benefit to be increasing at a fast pace.

J. Interest

The amount the insurance company charges you when you borrow their money. Yes, you are borrowing THEIR money; your cash value is the collateral. Borrowing against your cash value has an interest cost usually between 5 percent and 8 percent, depending on the company. In our research, we've found it doesn't really make as much difference as you'd think. The lower loan interest rate that life insurance companies often use is a variable rate (versus a fixed, but higher interest rate). See also the "direct recognition" section at the end of the glossary.

Do you want the companies you do business with to be profitable? Do you think insurance companies, banks, mortgage companies, and brokerage firms move their money all the time versus putting it in accounts and letting it sit there for 30 years? Since you probably answered *yes* to both questions, let's think about *why* the insurance company charges you interest when you borrow against your cash value or CLUE account. The most common question is, "Why do I have to pay interest to use my own money?" The answer is, you don't.

You can withdraw your money out of the life insurance net-cash-value account and go on your way. *Or* you can leave your money in there to grow and borrow the insurance company's money collateralized by your cash value, similar to a CD-secured loan. You pay the insurance company an interest rate for the use of their money. The cash-value account is yours to do as you want. The insurance company will pay you dividends on your policy based on the gross cash value, regardless of whether there is a loan against the cash value or not. If you choose not to collateralize your account and get it to do more jobs (see page 10), the insurance company will collateralize it among their general account assets and use it to do many jobs for them.

"Why pay 8 percent to a life insurance company when I can borrow at 6 percent from a bank?" you may ask. Micro-economically, looking at the question in a vacuum, you shouldn't. But *macro*-economically, looking at the big picture, sometimes paying a higher interest rate is worth the increase in flexibility. Since you control the loan at the life insurance company (unlike at the bank or car dealership), choosing to pay 8 percent gives you freedom and flexibility to skip payments or take longer if necessary to pay it back. Not that you should, but at least you have the freedom to.

"Why pay 15 percent back to my insurance company when they only charge me 8 percent?" If the marketplace is charging 15 percent for an equipment loan, yet you can borrow at 8 percent, then paying the 7 percent difference to your policy in the form of a manual paid-up addition will enable you to profit from the financing deal like a bank would. You can literally pay the difference every month or save it up and add it annually. True Family Banking (see phase 5) would require that 7 percent difference to be fair and square with the marketplace, which is where your economy operates.

K. Owner

This is usually the person who pays the premium, definitely the only person who can borrow against the cash value and control all of the working parts, and often (but not always) the insured.

L. Insured

The person upon whom the policy is written. When this person dies the death benefit is paid. If the insured is not the owner, the insured does not have any rights to the policy. However, the owner may give the policy to the insured at some point in the future without any transfer for value. (Think about starting this type of policy on your child for a future gift.)

M. Automatic premium loan

It may go by a different name at different companies, but this feature can help you in times of cash-flow challenges by literally recycling cash value to pay premiums and then increasing the cash value. It works the same way as a regular loan, but instead of the money going to you, the money goes to the life insurance company to pay the premium so your cash value increases and your loan increases. It's a strategy to use for a few years while you get back on track, not one to use forever.

N. Reduced paid-up

This is the "end of the rope" savior in the event that cash flow simply dies and you don't see a light at the end of the tunnel for many years. The insurance company reduces your death benefit and makes your policy "paid up" so no more premiums are required nor allowed. It's not a strategy you can undo, but it will keep you from losing the money you've paid in so far.

O. Opportunity cost

Opportunity cost is what you lose when you let dollars go unnecessarily to a financial institution or the government. Paraphrasing Heymann and Bloom in *Opportunity Cost in Finance and Accounting*, "the value of a resource is determined by its use in the best alternative given up." Remember Mark & Mary's story about educating their children from page 3? If they had used a 529 plan, they would have given that money to the college and it would have been gone — causing themselves a large opportunity cost because that money and all its growth was at the college instead of in their own accounts. However, by borrowing against life insurance cash value or real estate to pay for their children's education, Mark and Mary can educate their children *and* keep the asset growing.

A Note on Direct Recognition

There are two different methods insurance companies use to handle the loaned cash value — direct recognition and non-direct recognition. In a non-direct recognition company, the earnings rate on cash value is totally unaffected by any loans against cash value. In a direct recognition company, the earnings rates on loaned cash value are affected both positively and negatively when the cash value is used as collateral.

Generally, the loaned cash value has a dividend rate that is a certain number of basis points lower than the interest charged on the loan. So if the current-dividend-crediting rate is less than the direct-recognition-crediting rate, then the cash value is affected positively. If the current-dividend-crediting rate is greater than the direct-recognition-crediting rate, then cash value is affected negatively.

For example, let's say the current-dividend-crediting rate is 6.5 percent, and the loan rate is 8 percent with all loaned cash value getting a "100 basis point" (1 percent) reduction from the loan rate (bringing it down to 7 percent). That being the case, since 7 percent is obviously greater than 6.5 percent, borrowing against your cash value actually improves your situation because your dividend-crediting rate will be at 7 percent for the borrowed cash value and 6.5 percent for the non-borrowed cash value.

After all the analysis we've done on many companies and policies, we've found either way works just fine. Maybe consider having both!

Conclusion

We've discussed the three major areas of living your life insurance. The first is using the cash value from age 1 to age 81 or so. The cash value can stay in the policy and be your liquid "peace of mind account" or be borrowed against and used for other kinds of leveraged opportunities or investments.

Then, depending on age, health, and other financial instruments you have at the time, you switch focus to the death benefit, generally around age 75 or 80 or even 90. And you literally live your life insurance by using the death benefit while you are living. The seven strategies we covered in that section can be used alone or combined with each other to produce an income stream that is usually higher, due to less tax, than you could have without the life insurance death benefit.

Finally, we have given you a glossary of terms in plain English so you can truly understand what those statements from your life insurance company mean. And you'll know how to ask for what you want if you end up dealing with an 800-number rep (because the person who sold you the policy is no longer around). It is so important to keep policies in force, and in order to do that, you must understand what is happening to them. Since this is one financial product you will literally use your whole life (hence the name of the product) you will want to take the time to learn all the working parts.

You'll now start to see life insurance differently. Not as something for dying, but as something for living. Not as a policy to sit in a drawer, but as a tool to be used to make your life better. It's something to be funded and used, not denigrated and viewed as a necessary evil.

If you have questions about how to make this work for you, get back to the person who referred you to this e-book. Or if you are a client of Partners for Prosperity, Inc., call us at 877-889-3981 or visit us at www.partners4prosperity.com and ask for a review.

We close our e-book with the following quotation from *The Richest Man in Babylon* by George S. Clason:

The sixth cure, of seven — "insure a future income"

Surely when such a small payment made with regularity doth produce such profitable results, no man can afford not to insure a treasure for his old age and the protection of his family, no matter how prosperous his business and investments may be.

I would that I might say more about this. In my mind rests a belief that some day wise-thinking men will devise a plan to insure against death whereby many men pay in but a trifling sum regularly, the aggregate making a handsome sum for the family of each member who passeth to the beyond. This do I see as something desirable and which I could highly recommend. But today it is not possible because it must reach beyond the life of any man or any partnership to operate. It must be as stable as the king's throne. Some day do I feel that such a plan shall come to pass and be a great blessing to many men, because even the first small payment will make available a snug fortune for the family of a member should he pass on.

But because we live in our own day and not in the days which are to come, must we take advantage of those means and ways of accomplishing our purposes. Therefore do I recommend to all men that they by wise and well thought-out methods do provide against a lean purse in their mature years. For a lean purse to a man no longer able to earn or to a family without its head is a sore tragedy. This then is the sixth cure for a lean purse: Provide in advance for the needs of thy growing age and the protection of thy family.

Additional Reading

Pirates of Manhattan, Barry Dyke, 555 Publishing, 2007

Becoming Your Own Banker: Unlocking the Infinite Banking Concept, R. Nelson Nash, Infinite Banking, 2006

Beyond Majority Thinking: Helping Remove Uncertainty from Your Financial Future, Ronald Schutz, SMART Press, 2002

Learning to Avoid Unintended Consequences, Leonard Renier, Infinity Publishing, 2003

The Richest Man in Babylon: The Success Secrets of the Ancients, George S. Clason, Signet Publishing, 1988

Opportunity Cost in Finance and Accounting, H.G. Heymann and Robert Bloom, Quorum Books, 1990

Killing Sacred Cows: Overcoming the Financial Myths That Are Destroying Your Prosperity, Garrett Gunderson and Stephen Palmer, Greenleaf Book Group LLC, 2008

About the Author

KIM D. H. BUTLER has been a highly successful leader in the field of financial services since 1988. She first learned the value of work growing up on a farm in Oregon. In fact, Kim milked cows to put herself through private college. Whatever the circumstance, she has a gift for creating alternative ways to succeed. She is now a Kolbe Certified consultant, owner of Partners For Prosperity, Inc. and MountainTopsEducation.com, and a Coach for the Strategic Coach Program.

Kim is also the founder of The Prosperity Pathway™, which offers five steps to implement the 7 Principles of Prosperity™. She is able to use her ability to spot relevant patterns and issues to help her clients understand and utilize these principles. She also enables other Prosperity Economic Advisors to use The Pathway™ and The Principles™.

When Kim isn't busy strategizing with her clients, she puts her energy and skillful stamina to good use by enjoying time with her family, hiking, working on husband Todd Langford's alpaca farm, and reading.

Lastly, Kim thanks Bobby Mattei, Andrea Lazerus, and many other colleagues for their help in making this book better.

• • • • •

To receive personalized instruction on how to implement the product (what you buy) and the strategies (what you do) in this book, please contact Bobby Mattei at 318-861-2552 or Bobby@My-MountainTops.com.